Table of Contents

In *Open Window*, Henri used bright, bold colours instead of lifelike colours. Through the window, boats can be seen floating on pink waves.

4

Henri Matisse

Henri Matisse (1869–1954) is known for working with many art forms.
He painted, sculpted and made **etchings**. Henri also worked with new art forms. **Decoupage** is an art form that Henri helped make popular. It involves cutting pieces of coloured paper into shapes. Artists then arrange the shapes to make designs.

Henri led the **Fauves**. This group of artists painted with bright, bold colours to show feelings in their art.

Henri believed that art did not have to look lifelike. He showed people that art does not have to look real to be beautiful. His ideas changed the way people look at and create art.

Henri a famous French artist. He was also a very unusual person. One story says he liked to drive slowly down the middle of the road, blocking traffic. He drove this way so he could enjoy looking at the trees along the street.

Still lifes are paintings of objects. Artists sometimes paint still lifes to practise using colour and shading. Henri painted this still life *The Bottle of Schiedam* in 1896.

Young Henri

Henri was born in Le Cateau, France, on 31st December 1869. While growing up, he did not plan to be an artist. In 1887, he went to law school in Paris. A year later, Henri got a job in a law office. He did not think his work was very exciting.

In 1890, Henri became sick with appendicitis. His mother gave him a set of paints to keep him busy while he was in the hospital.

At first, Henri copied famous paintings. He then made his own works of art. His first painting was of a river and a mill. For fun, he signed it with his name written backwards, essitaM.

Art excited Henri. He took art classes in the morning before going to work. He also visited museums to see famous works of art.

In 1891, Henri left his job and moved to Paris to study art. He also wanted to learn from the many well-known artists who lived in Paris.

Woman Reading was one of Henri's first paintings shown at the Salon. The Salon's judges liked to pick traditional paintings with lifelike images and dark backgrounds.

Art Studies

Henri began his studies at the Academie Julian. His teachers taught a traditional painting style. This style used dark colours and lifelike images. Henri quickly grew bored with his studies. He wanted to develop his own way of painting.

In 1892, Henri began to study with Gustave Moreau. Moreau was a famous artist who taught at The École des Beaux-Arts in Paris. He encouraged Henri to find his own way of painting. He also told Henri to study old paintings. Artists learn how to paint by studying famous works of art.

While studying with Moreau, Henri became a father. In 1894, Caroline Joblaud gave birth to his daughter, Marguerite. Henri and Caroline never married.

In 1896, Henri's studies were rewarded. Some of his paintings were shown at the Salon in Paris. People from around the world came to see and buy art here and Henri sold two of his paintings.

The Dinner Table (above) was one of Henri's first attempts at **Impressionism**. People at the Salon did not like this painting because it looked blurry. Girl with Umbrella (right) was painted in the **Pointillist** style.

Art Styles

In 1897, Henri began to study new art styles. First, he studied **Impressionism**. Impressionists did not worry about painting lifelike pictures. They wanted to show how something looked at a quick glance. They used broken brush strokes of solid colours. Up close, their paintings look like they are covered with dabs of paint. But from a distance, a picture can clearly be seen.

While studying Impressionism, Henri married Amélie Parayre. She and Henri had two sons, Jean and Pierre. Amélie also helped to raise Marguerite.

During this time, Henri did not sell many paintings. Amélie opened a hat shop to support their family. She earned money so Henri could spend his time painting.

In the early 1900s, Henri studied **Pointillism**. Pointillists use small dots of colour to paint. Up close, the dots can be seen clearly in their paintings. From a distance, the dots blend together to form a picture.

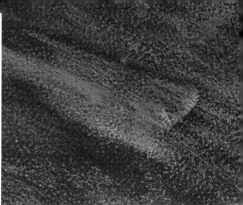

Henri painted a green stripe down the woman's face in *The Green Stripe (Madame Matisse)*. The stripe shows a clear line between light and shadow on her face. Henri displayed this Fauvist painting in 1905.

Fauvism

With Impressionism and Pointillism, Henri worked using bright, solid colours. This led Henri to develop his own style of painting and he stopped painting objects in lifelike colours. Instead, he used colours to show feelings in his art. Red might show excitement. Orange might show love.

In 1905, Henri displayed his work with other artists who used colours in similar ways. At first, people thought these artists were mad. People called them "les fauves," or "the wild beasts," because of their wild use of colour. Later, people called these artists **Fauvists**. Many people were interested in their new art style and Henri became rich selling his Fauvist paintings.

Henri continued to change his painting style as he worked. He began to paint objects in simple, flat shapes. He often painted the objects in one solid colour. He also stopped using the bright colours of his earlier Fauvist paintings.

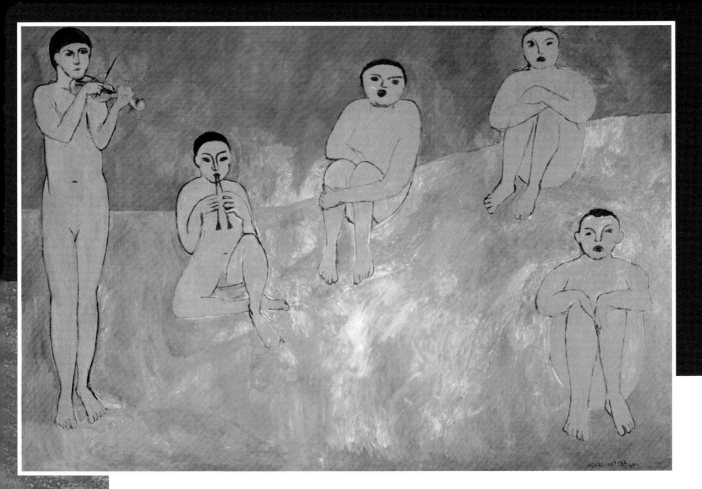

Henri used three main colours to paint the people and background in *Music*. He also did not give the people many details. He made this painting simple to create a peaceful scene.

Post-Impressionism

In 1908, Henri finished *Harmony in Red* (shown on front cover). This painting shows how his style had changed. Henri used bright colours, but objects in the painting did not look real. They looked flat.

Russian art collector Sergei Shchukin bought *Harmony in Red*. People in Paris called him the "Mad Russian" because he liked new and unusual art. In 1909, Shchukin hired Henri to paint *Dance* and *Music*. Over time, Shchukin bought nearly 40 of Henri's paintings.

In 1910, British art expert Roger Fry held an art exhibition in London. Art by Paul Cézanne, Georges Seurat, Paul Gauguin, Vincent van Gogh, and Henri were shown. These artists had different styles, but they all painted objects in colours and shapes that were not lifelike. Fry called them **Post-Impressionists** because these artists had once painted in the Impressionist art style. After Impressionism, they began working with new styles, like Fauvism.

un moment di libes.
Ne devrait-on
pas faire ac.
complir un
grand voyage
en avion aux
jeunes gens
ayant terminé
leurs études.

54

This page from Henri's book *Jazz* shows a picture called *Icarus*.
Henri made the original picture with coloured pieces of paper.

Moving to the Mediterranean

In 1917, Henri moved his family to Nice, France. This city is near the Mediterranean Sea. There, Henri painted scenes of the sea. Some of his works were also of women.

While in Nice, Henri worked on many projects. He made statues like *Seated Nude* and *The Back*. He made 29 drawings called etchings for Stephane Mallarme's book *Poesies*. Henri also made etchings for *Ulysses* a novel by James Joyce. He even made the costumes and set for a ballet called *Rouge de Noir*.

In 1947, Henri published *Jazz*. In this book, Henri wrote about his thoughts on life and art. The book included many brightly coloured pictures. Henri said he created these pictures by "drawing with scissors." He cut pieces of paper, painted them in different colours, and arranged them in patterns. This art form became known as **decoupage**.

Henri designed the altar (centre) and stained glass windows (left) for the Chapel of Saint-Marie du Rosaire in Vence. He also painted **murals** on the church's walls.

Final Years

In the early 1940s, Henri had an operation to remove cancer from his stomach. He never fully recovered. For the rest of his life, he spent a great deal of time in bed.

Henri did not let his illness stop him from working. At one point, he tied a piece of chalk to a stick. He used it to draw on the walls and ceiling of his room. Much of Henri's later artwork was made while working in bed.

In 1947, an official from the Chapel of Saint-Marie du Rosaire in Vence, who had once nursed him, visited Henri. She persuaded Henri to help decorate the church and he agreed to make stained glass windows. He also designed an altar, furniture and robes for the priests.

On the church's walls, Henri painted several **murals**. He wanted to keep these paintings simple. He outlined people and objects in black paint. He did not fill the paintings in with many details. Henri hoped the simple pictures would be understood by everyone.

Henri sculpted *La Serpentine* in 1909. Even in his statues, he used few details to show people.

Matisse's Fame

During the last years of his life, Henri was often ill. But he continued to make art. He designed stained glass windows, sculpted and worked with decoupage until his death. Henri died on 3rd November 1954. He was 84.

Henri greatly changed people's ideas about art. His work with different art styles taught people that art did not have to be realistic in colour and shape. He showed that colours and simple shapes could show meaning.

Henri also helped develop new types of art. Fauvism showed feelings through colour, pattern and form. Decoupage is often used today to make decorations.

Henri's art is on display in museums around the world. The Museum of Modern Art in New York shows some of his work. Many of his paintings are at the Pompidou Centre in Paris, the Musée Matisse in Nice and the Pushkin Museum in Moscow.

Timeline

1869 - Henri is born in Le Cateau, France on 31st December.

1887 - Henri goes to law school.

1891 - Henri quits his job and moves to Paris, France, to study art.

1892 - Henri meets Gustave Moreau.

1894 - Henri's daughter Marguerite is born.

1896 - The Salon displays several of Henri's paintings.

1899 - Henri's son Jean is born.

1900 - Henri's son Pierre is born.

1905 - The Fauvist art movement begins.

1910 - Henri shows his work with the Post-Impressionists.

1914 - World War I begins; the war ends in 1918.

1917 - Henri and his family move to Nice, France.

1939 - World War II begins; the war ends in 1945.

1947 - Henri publishes *Jazz*, a book about his thoughts on art and life.

1951 - Henri finishes the stained glass windows, murals, and furniture for the Chapel of Saint-Marie du Rosaire.

1954 - Henri dies of a heart attack on 3rd November.

Useful Websites

www.centrepompidou.fr/
english
Official site for The
Pompidou Centre in France,
a great source of pictures for
you to download.

www.moma.org
The Museum of Modern Art
in New York provides this
website for users to view
their galleries online. It
includes a good collection
of Matisse's works.

www.tate.org.uk
Official site for The Tate
Gallery in London. This
includes information on all
work held there and news
about upcoming exhibitions.

www.artbma.org/education/
matisse_kids_frame.html
Lively exploration of
Matisse's bold colourful
pictures, with the help of the
artist's dog Raoudi. You can
create your own Matisse
pictures and learn all about
the artist.

Note to parents and teachers
Every effort has been made by the
Publishers to ensure that
these websites are suitable for
children; that they are of the
highest educational value, and
that they contain no
inappropriate or offensive
material. However, because of the
nature of the Internet, it is
impossible to guarantee that the
contents of these sites will not be
altered. We strongly advise that
Internet access is supervised by a
responsible adult.

Glossary

altar - a large table used for religious ceremonies
appendicitis - a disease of the appendix; the appendix is a small, closed tube attached to the large intestine.
decoupage - the art of decorating with coloured cutouts of paper
etching - a picture created on a metal plate; an artist uses an etching to make prints of a picture.
Fauvism - an art movement using bright, bold colours to show feelings
Impressionism - an art style in which artists painted in broken brush strokes
mural - a large painting on a wall or a ceiling
Pointillism - an art style using small dots of colour
Still life - paintings of objects such as food or furniture

Index